Happenstance and Miracles

*For Helene
with love
and appreciation*

Love, Dawn

poems by

Dawn McDuffie

6-10-18

Finishing Line Press
Georgetown, Kentucky

Happenstance and Miracles

ACKNOWLEDGMENTS

Bear River Review, "Angels and Promises"
Literal Latté, "O Twinkie Moon"
Minerva Rising, "Consider the Turnip"
Quill & Parchment, "Getting There"
Third Wednesday, "Abalone Button," "All for Magic," "Fear," "Inner City," "It
Took Six People a Month to Pack that House," "Mixing Bowls," "Natural
Pearl," "On the Possibilities of Human Flight," "Origami," "To make a Demon
Trap Bowl," "To the Sunlight Radiant," "Welcome To the Canfield Bridge,"
"With Thankfulness"
Water Music, "Inner City"

Publisher: Leah Maines
Editor: Christen Kincaid
Cover Art and Design: Jonathan McDuffie
Author Photo: Jonathan McDuffie

Printed in the USA on acid-free paper.
Order online: www.finishinglinepress.com
also available on amazon.com

Author inquiries and mail orders:
Finishing Line Press
P. O. Box 1626
Georgetown, Kentucky 40324
U. S. A.

Table of Contents

for Jonathan

Natural Pearl

I had forgotten how pearl buttons rejoice
when slipped from a tight buttonhole.
Button, from the French word for bud,

pearl for mother of pearl, a shell already shining
with nacre, ready to glaze the alien parasite
with layers of shimmering white. No shimmer

without injury. An oyster knows irritation
and seals itself away, untroubled, a marriage
of beauty and layered protection.

Imagine a summer dress, cotton fine as silk.
Twenty buttons line up down the back, and
someone's patient hand must twist each one,

align, unfasten, move on to the next,
undressing slow as growth.

To Make a Demon Trap Bowl

Take a plain bowl, buff clay, no decorations.
Keep it empty—no buttons or keys—no money.
Draw the demon in chains at the bottom. It will never
be free. Name it jealousy, dementia, hopeless sadness.
Write the amulet of protection around the tormentor
in your best calligraphy—Aramaic or Greek—then write
more magical incantations in an upward spiral
until you almost reach the edge. Draw a perfect line
around the rim. Dig a hole under your doorway,
and bury the bowl. Repair the sandstone doorstep,
patch the porch. The evil eye will not find you.
Your own envy will never escape.

On the Possibilities of Human Flight

To fly was to pump the swing set to its highest point
and jump off—terrible jolt for a second of weightlessness—

or ride a bike cross town to our only hill, stand on pedals, push,
reach the top, and feel how fear changed my heart coasting down.

Sopranos sang with weightless voices, and I tried,
my darker voice tethered by gravity. To worship flight

is to worship gravity. My favorite poem, *To Earthward,*
for me, not about death, but lovemaking in an orchard,

all the leaves and sharp little twigs pressing into
those vulnerable bodies. At 27 I studied Aikido,

and Sensei sometimes picked me to demonstrate his throw,
then judged the smoothness of my obedient arc across the mat.

I wanted to fly straight from his fingertips, to align heart
and body, air resistance shaping my readiness and forward roll.

I dedicated one practice session to a friend, dead with no
warning the day before. *Watch*, I told her.

*This is how life unfolds—heaven and earth—love
and that dirty bicycle chain, indifference.* I swear

I floated through falling, getting up, falling again
until it was my turn to spin another person into air.

Getting There

Exit where rose-colored day lilies flood the median
of I-94, and turn right on the first nondescript road.
Pass Billy's Wedding Chapel. Turn left at a street

named after a tree you remember—Beech—
its smooth bark carved with a heart that encloses
your name. From vacant lots that dot the street,

space settles on your skin. Children cool off
in a spray of water and rainbow, then run
to help Dad polish the car for Sunday.

You are lost, but you don't want to leave
this half memory. There are no stores nearby,
but there might be a river close, willows not too far.

The Fellowship of Freedom and Grace sells chicken
dinners or ribs with potato salad, coleslaw, peach
cobbler and iced tea, every plate blessed by the cook.

Trees here are older than childhood. Maple,
Hickory, and Oak cast islands of shade
on porches and front lawns, and shimmering heat

turns tall grasses into optical illusions. You feel an insect's
buzz as if it came from your throat, but it is only your body's
steady hum. Prairie Smoke, Cardinal Vine, and Larkspur

explode like fireworks between houses—back yards
overgrown with waves of purple Hollyhocks and
Queen Anne's Lace, flowers sometimes called weeds.

What the Moon Says About My Shoes

You don't have a choice.
Not with those feet—proud and demanding
at the arch, flat and hopeless
behind the toes—they hate bondage.
I see you walk on polished concrete,
cinders, lake stones, oak boards
that moan, especially at 3:00 a.m.
You will never wear glass pumps,
but remember my opal sandals
walk everywhere and trouble the twin hearts
of right and left. I leave no footprint
but a cool spot small as a nickel.
Your mean little shoes, rigid and dead,
shoes that resist lining up at night—
I'm watching them for you.

Angels and Promises

Mom said angels have heels, but she never explained
what she meant. I wondered what other details angels
hid under those floating robes. Why did filmy gowns
ride flat on angelic shoulders with a slit just big enough
for a wing joint but way too small for the huge sweep
of muscular feathers? Do angels have heels to walk
in step with humans, to balance, kneeling to Mary
as she hears the good news? Does Raphael, angel
in disguise, need a human foot to walk with Tobias from
Nineveh to Rages? Could Tobias's little dog nip at the
angel's heels, if angels didn't have heels? Although
in truth, heels are not needed to make forgiveness
more attractive than revenge. You'd want an angel
of that sort to hover close to you, parallel to the earth,
with no bit of human weight or bulk to distract you.
But the angels who speak to you fight gravity like a novice
swimmer treading water. They thrash in the air.
One at your right ear says, *Believe the great promises.*
Its right heel clips your shin and leaves a wedge shaped
bruise. The one at your left ear caresses your ankle
with the beating pulse of its heel as it chants, *Oh
Beloved, nothing is certain in this world except
happenstance and miracles. Promises are for liars.*

Fear

In my own house at 3:00 a.m., the queasy part
of night, small dangers magnify themselves. I clutch
a banister—gasp when the hall light sparks out.
I know an extra step sprouts between the second

floor and the landing when I am weak, night blind.
Those nights when I cannot sleep, the quest for water
is insurmountable, the kitchen so far from my bedroom.
A light switch moves to a new location, and I can't

find the connections in my mind, my faith in thinking.
I exhale and the names fly out. I wait for repair—wait
for the click of a name that flies back to me. Sometimes
it works, or maybe the sky darkens and nothing returns.

October Snow Incites Every Leaf to Die

The Peace Rose, shaken by last night's storm,
sticks to her summery ways, coral and cream
all shrouded in white. Ophelia lies wreathed
with flowers in her damp wedding dress.
She's far too cold to get up and demand
a slice of whiskey-cake. Our familiar orb spider
suspended in the twisted cherry tomato vine
sits very still, her snappy black and yellow
bright as ever despite tonight's predicted frost.

Consider the Turnip

I want the soup of making do, soup of good
enough, bitterness I disguise with spice
and salt with expectations, my hunger
specific. I want vegetables that taste like
dirt, crooked carrots, potatoes staring
at me from their lair, and gleaming turnips.
Although turnips are living opals, sweet
and earthy, they will not make me important.
I will never be rich. No one knows my name.
I pour in lentils, stony as little teeth
and simmer all of it like a grievance.
Then, much later, I turn off the fire.

Origami

I need a paper crane, blazing
red and gold, willing to flap its wings.
I'm so tired of carrying my dull heart
from morning coffee through the cloudy veil
of afternoon. Who needs practical questions?
I'd rather fold this small flame in the crown of light
that surrounds earth, the invisible aurora borealis
that blesses any object with no goal beyond beauty.

Paper Airplane

Today she can't find her purse and its clutter of identification,
used tissues, a small picture book she wants to give a child.
And she can't remember which child—her youngest daughter's girl
or those kids in Arizona? Any child might need a book.
Just thinking of the lost name of a girl or boy starts the hiccups.
Someone is lonely. Her identification is lost and that's the end of it.
If bodies are made of water, souls are made of memory. Can that
be right? She hopes not, because whole decades winked out today
like headlights in a used sedan. She knows an empty envelope
sent through U.S. Mail is a paper airplane of hate. Remember
that movie where miners trapped in a collapsed tunnel
saw their lanterns darken? First one sputtered, then another,
and the screen turned into a blizzard of black and white fragments.

To the Sunlight Radiant

in the east window:
Go away. I hate
my house, too clean,
my mind empty as
a used egg. Any day
my fraud will be
exposed. I want
everything back
I've given away.

With Thankfulness

for predators
with 5 foot wing spans—
they want me: blood,
lungs, every gristled
bit. For protection: pearl
big as my thumb, yellow
thread blessed
by the Dalai Lama,
wool socks hand knit
like Pablo Neruda's socks.
For theory, theology,
coffee every morning,
out of print books
that arrive in a week.
For dark chocolate
in the cupboard
and daily mail.
For the malicious class of 1967
waiting 50 years for revenge.
For mystery: charms that
don't work, invisible change.
For feeling alone.
For clothes that keep my secrets,
friends who don't tell.

Inner City
     After Pablo Neruda

A wind from 1900 ruffles the ruined mansions of Woodbridge,
carrying fragments of gold and emerald glass, a decent wage
torn into street confetti, gravel beating on burned out houses—

upper flat for the family, lower flat to pay the mortgage.
How can the streets stay clean when dead men gather on corners
and throw phantom beer cans into dusty green foundation shrubs?

At the illegal shelter men flop on exercise mats, glad to be this far
from rain's insistent teasing. Although the skylight is large enough,
the moon never comes inside and her pure little sisters left Detroit

a century ago. Tree of Heaven grows in the neighbor's gutter;
Belladonna with its evil rubies twines through cyclone fencing.
Who knows what happened to Mrs. Purdy? Her kitchen exhaled

biscuits every weekend. She is not here, and her house has tumbled
into itself, roof flown away to its afterlife. Her prosperous little garden
runs to weeds and poison, and vandals have stolen her potting shed.

Escaped parakeet, blue as a Thunderbird convertible, circles the trees
for a place where freedom burns warm as captivity. Poor dreamer's
body weighs less than an ounce, and no one will see it in the vacant lot

so thick with ghosts and regret. No child will line a cardboard box
or bury it where Feverfew and Queen Ann's Lace protect what earth
has claimed. Other residents wait: nightmares, rats, feral dogs.

All for Magic

Caro Elementary School, grades one through six. I was transfixed
by light and what made it happen—chips of silver or sequins.
Marionettes put on their clothes behind a black plush curtain
where winter stars gleamed and disappeared as we waited.

Were there holes in the velvety folds? The curtain trembled,
and I didn't know what a puppet show was or what might
hide behind the sparkle. I wanted every shiny thing—sugar crystals
on sugar cookies, silver cap gun, secrets, my own tambourine.

All for magic: grace of wasps, speed of a blue racer flowing
from hand to hand like a living Slinky, my small soul following
his glittering blue into a house of weeds. I couldn't stop
searching for gems in plain rock, or a word to make it true.

Welcome to the Canfield Bridge

Graffiti artists have dedicated every inch
to the tricky muses of peace and war. I read

Welcome to the Canfield Bridge. A stenciled
heart and *Hell Smoke* nestle together.

Someone turned every crack into a daisy stem—
all these years and still daisies everywhere.

It's good to walk with nothing but air in my hands,
a house-key in my pocket. Those stoned saints

of the 1970s may have been right when they said,
Walk with empty hands. Carry nothing into the world.

Four blocks to my left, sugar-pink peonies flaunt
their petals until the first hard rain. Two blocks east,

four beehives line the border of a weedy lot,
and dried sunflower heads stand ready for cardinals.

It Took Six People a Month to Pack That House

Good-bye to the German children. Their downcast
mouths kissed last week's newspaper. I wrapped
bells, crystal clappers padded with tissue, china Scotties
small as a fingernail, a tray of funeral jewelry woven
from hair, Bo-peep, eight inches high and hollow, heavy
for her size, all her feelings trapped under the glaze.
Then transferware, nurse dolls, a bust of Teddy Roosevelt.
We love what we love. The daughter wrapped 25 rooms
of dollhouse armoires and single beds, commodes,
tablecloths, but she grew up before she unpacked.
Detroit, Twin Cities, Cincinnati, Toledo—another place
pulled and the family followed. Sweet grass baskets
and colored glass followed. A parlor organ with
mouse holes in its lungs could barely keep up.

O Twinkie Moon

your yellow halo of ice crystals
might mean snow before morning

or moon confections, pale cakes—
cream filling made of oil and imagination.

Science, pages of algorithms,
and the tasty gifts of chemistry

cannot drive out metaphor;
I thank you, tender moon.

My coffee cup longs for tomorrow,
for reliable inspiration, perfection.

O Twinkie Moon, my quarters rattle
in the cosmic vending machine,

and I punch your number, bite
the sweet replica one more time.

Mixing Bowls:

Heavy stoneware, yellow with a brown stripe,
ivory with a peach strip, or my favorite, a creamy blue,
crayon box blue whipped up with white as if the bowl
had created a place of alchemy in its hollow interior.

On New Year's Eve, 1972, I'm stirring frizzled
chicken liver, rendered chicken fat, onions fried
to transparency. I want transmutation, an elixir
that turns every object in the kitchen golden.

I taste and stir, take another taste, add salt.
I have found my lover and I will feed him pâté
and apple crisp. I set the blue bowl aside to chill,
and I peel fruit into the yellow bowl humming,

comfort me with apples, and do not stir up...love
until it is ready. But truly, without stirring, how will love
be ready? I can't go into the city and pick mushrooms
for dinner, blackberries for dessert. I buy what I need,

and transform it with fire, with spice, with long
mixing in a bowl. Every apple grows from remixed
soil, recycled water. *There is nothing new under the sun,*
the Preacher said, but this feels fresh, hot and fragrant.

Abalone Button

shines like the moon come back to earth to dedicate itself to a monastic life. It promises to hold together two halves or two opposites. Button holds at your will and releases at your will, not knowing the tricks of human hands, the sideways approach to a border or tightly embroidered buttonhole. Poor button, fabricated for the utility of others. It has two holes to welcome binding threads and the needle that delivers them. Sweet button, I dreamed you shone in the sky again, bright and single, deep as your daughters, all of them pearls. I dreamed you were my glistening heart holding spirit to body.

In *Happenstance and Miracles* **Dawn McDuffie** explores an inner landscape of memory, imagination and dreams. This more imagistic sensibility reveals aspects of life frequently hidden from casual observers. Her poems have appeared in *Rattle, The MacGuffin, Third Wednesday, Feminist Studies,* and the anthologies, *Mona Poetica,* edited by Diane DeCillis and Mary Jo Firth Gillett, and *Good Poems—American Places,* edited by Garrison Keilor. Her chapbook, *Carmina Detroit,* was published in 2006 by Adastra Press. Finishing Line Press published *Bulky Pick Up Day* in 2011, and a second Adastra chapbook, *Flag Day in Detroit,* was published in 2012. McDuffie has taught creative writing in Detroit since 2000.

CPSIA information can be obtained
at www.ICGtesting.com
Printed in the USA
LVHW01s0110080518
576364LV00001B/35/P

9 781635 344509